St Paul:
12 Steps to New Lif

Paul J Broadbent LLB(Hons).MA(Econ).MA

Acknowledgements

The reflections are entirely personal and prompted by life, family and prison chaplaincy experience.

They do not claim to be authoritative.

This process cannot be undertaken without the support and guidance of others, and as ever I would like to thank the special people who at various times and in their own way have advised and guided me.

Wanda

Emma

Laura

Andrew

Philip

Fr Martin Haigh OSB, formerly of Ampleforth Abbey (RIP)
Carolyn and Steve formerly @ HMP Lancaster Castle
and Shawn @ HMP Thorn Cross

Thank you and God bless each of you.

Copyright Acknowledgements

CONTENTS

"Still in Denial"   ....An Introduction to the 12 Steps

1 Songwriter...1 Scripture passage...1 Prisoner...1 Poem...1 Prison Chaplain

"Still in Denial"

You got a problem you won't admit
You got a habit that you can't kick
You're still in denial

Your wife is gone and you've grown old
The money's spent and the house is sold
You're still in denial

You've been living in a drunkard's dream
On a lost weekend, in a silent scream
I saw your picture in a photograph
You think it's funny but I still can't laugh, No

You gotta get it through your f..... up head
You gotta stop it or you'll drop down dead
You're still in denial

That love is something you don't understand
You won't accept a helping hand
Right now you're sinking in quicksand
You're still playing in a one-man band

You've been living in a drunkard's dream
On a lost weekend, in a silent scream
I saw your picture in a photograph
You think it's funny but I still can't laugh, no

You got a problem you won't admit
You got a habit that you can't kick
You're still in denial [1]

You may think that this is an odd way to introduce a guide which invites you to reflect upon passages from St Paul as a means of recovering, re-centering and redirecting your life.

"Still in denial" are the lyrics written by Gerry Rafferty, posthumously released in 2021 some ten years after his untimely death at the age of 63, primarily due to alcoholism.

But read the words again, sense his painful and humble acknowledgement of his condition. Consider his bravery amidst his brokenness. In fact, read, listen to any number of his heartfelt, heartbroken songs: Night Owl, The Right Moment, Don't give up on me, Hearts run dry, and Whatever's written in your heart. You will find a soul searching for answers to his own weakness, acknowledging the hurt being caused to himself and loved ones, and the loss being experienced as a consequence, but all the while from within a soul still searching for love.

"Still in denial" is a wake up call. The authoritative 12 Step Programme published in 1953 by the inspired founders of Alcoholics Anonymous is a guide to help victims address and respond to their condition. It has been adopted and adapted in many ways since to address all forms of addiction and many other debilitating psychological and health related conditions.

"I cannot understand my own actions. For I do not do the good that I want,   but the evil that I do not want, that is what I do..."   *... Romans 7 v 15-17*

St Paul here both acknowledges his weakness but also tries to understand why this may be and realises that he like you and I are all human and, as such, are all flawed.

Addictions, depression, anxiety and anger outbursts are all manifestations of the way that we as humans respond to the ups and downs of day to day life in a world which, let's admit, is getting increasingly difficult to live peacefully in.

Whether it be music, various programmes to recalibrate thinking and behaving, or guidance from Scripture, we all from time to time need to acknowledge where we are at, recognise and accept our weaknesses and, attempt to redress imbalances that we may find.

This reinterpretation of the 12 Step programme is simply offered as a way of asking you to consider the wisdom in the letters written by the hand and heart of St Paul as he wrestles with his own weakness and guides his readers to a different way of being in this earthly life.

The book is also written based upon the privilege of having served 12 years in Prison Chaplaincy, 12 years which gave an insight into the 12 Step and other recovery programmes and their potential to offer lifelines to people; 12 years where the sharing of various passages from St Paul with prisoners seemed to help bring about some transformations; 12 years which sadly saw people still in denial, or so broken by their addiction and life that the hope which flickered within was snuffed out by their own weakness or, often the darkness of others.

And so to conclude this introduction with the cautionary and heart breaking tale of Darryl and the poem that I treasure from him.

Whatever your addiction, your condition or your desperation, please allow Darryl's story, the 12 Steps and the passages from St Paul to act as some wake up call for you.

Don't stay "still in denial", do seize "the right moment" and, do respond to "whatever's written in your heart...that's all that matters".

Hope is an Angel – Darryl's Story

A constant theme throughout prison life generally are drugs and the impact of drugs on not only on people's physical and psychological welfare, but also their prospects for resettlement and readjustment to life.

There were two early and memorable contacts at HMP Thorn Cross with two different characters, each of whose personal life had been damaged by drugs.

The first of these was Daryll, who was a gentle, gifted artist in his late 30's when we met. He had clear blue eyes and meeting him, you sensed almost that you could see into his soul. Shawn, a gifted chaplaincy colleague, described him as "blessed, but broken"

His gentleness and brokenness could make your heart melt if you spent time with him and he personally divided his time between the Art Department producing some masterful pieces and in his room writing poetry.

Conversations with Daryll revolved mostly around his desperation to break the habit of drugs and the resulting cycle of being sent back to closed prison conditions. The habit had such a grip on his life that, whilst he engaged with the in-house Prison Pathways team, he always had the fear that the addiction could ruin his life.

Another constant theme of conversations was hope and how he was desperately trying to cling to the hope that he might one day satisfy the authorities that he was sufficiently clean to be considered eligible for release.

Daryll was one of a category of prisoners referred to as IPP's (Indeterminate sentence for public protection). In effect, this meant that he could be detained indefinitely until Probation inside and outside the prison, were satisfied that his behaviour was sufficiently controlled that he could be released without further risk to the community. Hence, this tragic balance between hope and fear which also played out in the minds and hearts of those others fortunate enough to meet this gentle, broken soul. In addition to being a gifted artist, Daryll loved to write poetry. I share a poem that he gave me one morning as I visited his room to catch up.

Hope

Hope is an exit
When you're stuck in a hole
Hope is a light
Deep down in your soul

Hope is a dream
When you're sleeping away
You wish not to wake
You're enjoying your stay.

Hope is an angel
that you don't want to touch
If she flies away
The pain is too much

So we hide from some hopes
They seem so far away
But my angel of hope
Will come back some day

Daryll

This puts into words the thoughts also of St Paul as he makes us aware of the constant struggle by many against the weaknesses and turmoil of human life. For some it is a constant struggle against a darkness that shrouds their life and blocks out, for the time being at least, the light of hope.

Darkness comes in many forms and addiction in its various guises is one. But then physical and psychological illnesses also bring darkness into the lives of many, as does abuse, anger, violence and poverty.

Because of our nature, some will suffer and struggle and endure, clinging to hope that may eventually see them through as stronger, more resilient, more rounded people with the real potential to help others similarly damaged by darkness.

St Paul realised that for some this desperate clinging to hope caused in itself further suffering because the end could not be seen.

Patience in Daryll's case was tragically balanced with fear and a desperation which affected his stability and, ultimately reduced his ability to cope with continuously clinging to the hope of release. Tragic it was because others around him supplied him with banned substances to allay his paranoia but this in due course caused him to fail a random drugs test.

Because of his IPP status, there was no flexibility or discretion offered by the Prison authorities and Daryll was sent back to closed conditions in the prison estate. Hope, at least for the near future hopefully, was snuffed out by the darkness of others actions and the weakness of Daryll.

Be honest now and ask yourself whether you need to change. When will be the moment that you choose to change. I can't do that for you, but I hope and pray for you, that you can.

Paul Broadbent... Chaplain... HMP Edinburgh

Knowing Me...

Have you ever sat crouched in the corner of a hallway with an old wall-mounted phone directly above you but not reached up to use it to call for help for fear of having a heart attack?

This was me.

Have you ever waited some three hours in that corner for your wife or partner to come home, only to re-assure you, or at least try to, that this is another panic attack?

This was me.

Have you ever been told in no uncertain terms by your GP that he has instructed staff not to make anymore urgent appointments for you, without first seeking his approval.

This was me.

Have you ever travelled down a third floor escalator in a department store, looked over and down to the basement and worried that you might just be tempted to fall?

This was me

Have you ever, after three years of cortisone racing through your body, so many sleepless nights, uncontrollable waves of panic attacks and phantom heart attack symptoms, finally laid back on a bed during daytime, cried out for help and suddenly sensed warmth, peace and some inexplicable light, the like of which you have never known before?

This finally, is me.

A version of me that I had not known for some time, during which I had been lost to myself and others close to me, who had supported, cared for and carried the lesser and seemingly powerless form of me.

Before we know it, and often without warning, each of us can at any point in our life become completely lost to ourselves, whether it be a health anxiety as in this case caused by multiple life triggers or whether it is alcohol, drugs, divorce, failure, fear, serious illness or tragedy.

CBT, counselling, mindfulness, relaxation all can take you so far but the key to transformation and renewal is accepting that you may be powerless, reaching out, acknowledging and accepting that you are loved not only here but somewhere beyond this time and place and then, being prepared to accept change and recognise previous failures and make apologies to casualties.

I didn't have the benefit of having read the 12 Steps programme, or the practical insights to life and spirituality in the letters of St Paul at the time. I so wish that I had, particularly the latter. But the final Step of the 12 Steps Programme calls on its participants to become ambassadors for change in the lives of others. St Paul too encourages much the same as he writes:

"God helps us in all our troubles, so that we are able to help others in any kind of trouble with the same help that we ourselves have been given ..."

...2 Corinthians 1 v 4

Over the last twelve years or so as a Prison Chaplain, with gratitude to my first guides Carolyn Woodcock and Steve Ball formerly of HMP Lancaster Castle and latterly Shawn Verhey at HMP Thorn Cross, I have had the privilege of putting some of the lessons that I learned into practice with prisoners that I have sat with as they shared their own journeys. These words of St Paul make so much more sense as you look back and then are able to share them to help others.

I acknowledge also Gavin Ball, formerly of HMP Lancaster Castle who first made me aware of the 12 Steps programme and, the lads then detained at the Castle who would gather in the Chaplaincy each Tuesday evening during association to take part in the AA 12 Step programme to bravely share their failures.

I place some of St Paul's writing at your feet as you take your first steps forward to transforming your own life.

"All God's holy people send you their blessings"

...2 Corinthians 13 v 12

...Knowing you!

"I cannot understand my own actions. The thing that I least want to do, that is what I do and that which I want to do, I do not do ..." ...Romans 7 v 15-17

The "12 Steps" and the "Big Book" were originally conceived between 1935 and 1953 when they were written by broker Bill W and surgeon Dr Bob S to share 18 years of helping chronic alcoholics manage their illness by encouraging self-acknowledgement, surrender, honesty and, apology.

The Steps themselves have been adapted over the years since as a means of addressing many different conditions and so, likewise here they are used as a map to guide the way to self-renewal.

But perhaps as importantly, it is useful to spend a little while looking at yourself, trying to really understand you and what has brought you to this point in your life.

Whatever it is that has brought you to this point, to the point where you now know that you have to do something about it, whether it be alcoholism, drugs, depression, grief, illness or any other number of health anxieties, you know that other people will have their opinions of you, your condition, your behaviour and even your future.

The thing is that only you and you alone know what is going on in your mind and how you have coped and responded to your thoughts and feelings. Others may listen, even sympathise with your pain, but it is you in your isolation and in the quietist moments that experience the turmoil and suffering that accompanies the pain. Suffering is yours and yours alone.

The way that you and your body have responded to the suffering have become your coping mechanism for better or for worse. But you deserve to do more than cope and now you have decided to do more. You need to do more than cope because coping is not living and that is what has brought you and countless others to this point of change.

These particular 12 Steps are hopefully just an invitation to consider along with the insights of St Paul, that there may be a spiritual path to change and renewal. But also that he too, as you will see in the first of the 12 Steps, brought himself to this point of asking: What is going on with me? What can I do about it? What am I going to do about it?

Read this passage now and in the next chapter we can take a closer look at it:

"I cannot understand my own actions. The thing that I least want to do, that is what I do and that which I want to do, I do not do ..."   *...Romans 7 v 15-17*

Can you hear the frustration that he feels with himself in what he writes? Do you not feel the same frustration? You may feel it, but time and again you have tried, maybe even reached out, but failed to make the change that St Paul knew he had to make.

If this is your suffering, your condition then only you can try and understand, only you can unpick what the possible causes are. Honestly, until you get to the root causes and take ownership of and responsibility for them, to the extent that you can, you are unlikely to move on or, find the inner strength to try.

So, it is time to be honest, but more than that, time to be kind to yourself and try to discover what might have caused you to suffer like this.

The original 12 Steps make constant reference to "God, or the higher power that you understand". Here, it should be pointed out that St Paul recognises only THE higher power of God and that is our starting point here. God though the power of His holy Spirit has the power to transform lives, to transform your life, if you are willing to place your trust in Him.

Take a look at yourself and your past to date in each of these three ways. Without it becoming too much like hard work, it might be useful to get pen and paper and think about your past, your upbringing, your lifestyle and put them down in front of you. For each of these three areas try to think about what you have faced, what you have thought, how you have felt and, how you have responded?

(See also the Appendix: Knowing You...some questions to help you)

Firstly in your life have you;

∞   Faced threats, challenges, dangerous situations, difficult situations?
How have you felt? How have you responded? How did you cope?
Has it been avoidance, anxiety, escape, survival or each of them?

∞   Next in your life have you been encouraged, pushed or self-driven to achieve goals, targets, status?
How has this made you respond?
Motivated? Positive? Over-powered? Deflated?

∞   Finally, throughout your life, have you felt cared for, valued and given time, encouragement and space to care for yourself?
How have your thoughts and feelings about yourself developed over time?
Have you felt cared for, calm, loved, safe?

Only you can know where the balance in these three areas lies in your life to date and, which has caused you to think and feel and act as you do. Without doubt though, somewhere in one of these areas lies the root of what has brought you to this place. There may be some form of suffering that only you know of which has prompted your mind, your body to respond in the way that it has.

Some of the causes may be outside of your control, some you have brought on yourself, but now without judgement and with care, compassion and kindness for yourself, you have to accept responsibility to alleviate your own suffering, to change what you can and instead to choose a better way of thinking, responding and living. You are being called to live a better life, a life that you deserve to live.

∞   ∞   ∞

This may have seemed a strange chapter to place in a journal which is encouraging a spiritual path towards change and renewal, but think about it for a moment, is it?

You, me, we all are absolutely unique, in make-up, mind, life and the way we respond to it. St Paul, along with all the scriptural writers, assures us that being unique, we are intimately known and loved by a Creator who cares for us and seeks only to be known by us.

In order to renew yourself then, let go of what has brought you to this place, what you have come to terms with, face and deal with the reality that you have lived and responded to, to date. It is learning how you have felt, thought and how you have responded up to now that will allow and enable you to make changes, face the challenges and experience the rewards of the new path that you are about set foot on.

Step 1:

Admit that you are powerless – that life has become unmanageable

"I cannot understand my own actions. For I do not do the good that I want, but the evil that I do not want, that is what I do..."   *... Romans 7 v 15-17*

Take a closer look at the words of St Paul. Not only is he acknowledging what he and countless writers before and since have acknowledged, but he is putting before us what we ourselves know to be the case at whatever point and situation in life we are at.

Life in many ways can be tragic. This is not to say that our life is a tragedy waiting to unfold. No, it is to acknowledge that life is unpredictable. With few exceptions, the course of any lifetime is a series of ups and downs.

What mattered to St Paul and what matters to you here and now is the realisation that this is just part and parcel of life, this precious but vulnerable life that each of us live. As powerless as you may feel even at your lowest point, you are not alone and life can change for you. As you embark on any 12 Step programme, you have to believe this is possible.

Mostly, we find that by taking rational, timely decisions despite unpredictability and uncertainty, we may be able to navigate a course through life which may bring us rewards, self-satisfaction, comfort and company. I hesitate to use the word happiness because that is subjective and for some may be unachievable. That too is the reality of some earthly lives.

Also besides the unpredictability of life, St Paul is recognising that for some who are not able to navigate an untroubled course, that life, circumstances and conditions can lead them to places where they feel out of control, powerless and searching for a way beyond. Some may feel they are in a place of helplessness, for others it is a constant state of hopelessness.

If at this point you still cling to the belief that as powerless and helpless as you are, you alone can make life manageable and that you can fix your life, then sadly and most likely, further pain is on the way. You have to accept as a probability that left to your own devices, life may well get worse or at least keep repeating itself. In order to create a distraction from the pain, it is likely that your addiction of choice, or necessity, will also get worse.

It would be easy and perhaps more comfortable but not at all satisfactory to gloss over what may bring any one of us to this place of seeming powerlessness. Better rather to name the causes and to acknowledge as St Paul did that these conditions exist because of our flawed human nature.

"It's easier to subdue an enemy without, than one within". [2]

Alcohol, drugs, death, serious illness, clinical depression and associated anxiety states, compulsive behaviours of every kind, controlling and passive aggressive behaviours, unemployment and related financial difficulties are just some of the flawed conditions that Steps One to Twelve are designed to help. Each of the circumstances can either cause or alternatively be the response to a life in chaos.

At any point in any of our lives, one or more of these troubling and tragic conditions may cast a shadow over our life. It is impossible to minimize the debilitating impact that these conditions can have on our ability to live, let alone function. Powerlessness is just one word to describe what it may be like to be caught in the vortex of one of these conditions.

Powerless and yet not hopeless. For many people and their families, friends and colleagues these are tragic situations and still, if we are people of faith, if we are or can become people with hope in the infinite, these finite tragic situations need not overcome us. This life will reach its natural conclusion one day, no matter how fortunate in it we may be. But for people of faith, hope lies beyond this finite life, in a place of peace beyond hopelessness and decline.

St Paul himself was no stranger to suffering and hardship. In the opening passage above, he openly admits to his human frailty and his pre-condition to constantly getting things wrong. You can almost sense his frustration as he wrestles within himself to try and do the right thing, to live righteously, but fails because like each of us he is weak and prone to repeating mistakes. He is powerless because he is human.

But despite this apparent powerlessness, he goes to a deeper place in himself to seek not only a strength within, but also to place his hope in a power without, a power that would transform his life and which he implores each of us to cast out into the depths to discover. He encourages us to hold onto hope even in the most tragic and seemingly hopeless circumstances.

Take time to read, to meditate upon and draw strength from the words that he writes to you in the depths of your own despair.

Powerless you may be at the moment, hopeless you are not. There is a power both within and beyond each of us, a power that listens to and understands our despair, but which also searches our depths to provide help.

"though we do not know how to pray, the Spirit intercedes for us in sighs too deep for words..."   *...Romans 8 v 27*

To summarise Step 1 then, despite the present chaos of your life, you have to cling to the belief that life can be better for you. Strangely by admitting that you are powerless, by accepting that you are weak, it is at that very point that you can become powerful, that you can reclaim the life that you were meant to live.

"I rejoice in weaknesses, in insults, in hardships, in persecutions, in difficulties. For when I am weak, then I am strong..."   *...2 Corinthians 12 v 10*

Step 1: Honesty

"It's easier to subdue an enemy without, than one within". [3]

Step 2:

Come to believe that a Power greater than yourself could restore you to sanity

> *"It is not as if you live in the dark (brothers) for that day to overtake you like a thief. No, we are all sons of the light and of the day. We do not belong to the darkness or to the night ..."*   ... *1 Thessalonians 5 v 4*

Time then for courage, humility, a leap of faith and hope in equal measures. It also takes a fair amount of risk and for many I guess, a step into the unknown possibly unwelcome territories of faith and spirituality.

Difficult too for those who struggle with issues of control and obsessive behaviour. How can it be right to surrender your life ahead to the unknown and intangible. What do I mean by God or my higher power anyway? How can I surrender to someone or something that I have never known or believed in? This is my life and the way I want to live it, so why should I?

Each of these are reasonable questions and positions to hold, and are perhaps only to be expected if you have never held a faith or, have consciously decided not to.

Read again the words of St Paul. Whilst this second step encourages you to let go, it necessarily still involves free choice. It is that choice of light rather than darkness, a move from powerlessness to a place of being empowered that you are being invited to choose.

The choice of light over darkness is a choice of life over death. See life as a rebirth of your former self, a choice of allowing what you have become to wither and die, allowing the self that you always wanted and were meant to be to rise to new life, to light.

As I write, this following passage came up in the Daily Readings and whilst it is not St Paul, it nevertheless is the received wisdom that he would have been grounded in during his formative years.

"I have set before you life and death, the blessing and the curse. Choose life then, that you and your descendants may live by loving the Lord your God, heeding his voice and holding fast to Him. For that will mean life for you, a long life"...

... 1 Deuteronomy 30 v 18 - 20

Strange isn't it that the next passage, the Gospel (Good News) of the day contains this line from the writing of St Luke.

"whoever loses his life for my sake, will save it"...   *... Luke 9 v 23-24*

The very act of letting go and trusting in God, the higher power of our Creator transforms darkness and loss into light and life if only you can let go and trust.

St Paul writes this:

"Do not be conformed to the pattern of this world but be transformed by the renewal of your mind that you may see what hope His call holds for you"...   *...Romans 12 v 2*

I love this idea of either being conformed or allowing ourself to be transformed. What would you want from your life now if it is in a place of brokenness? This world, our nature is determined by expectations, ways of being, patterns of thinking which lead to patterns of behaviour that the world in turn, accepts and expects.

But the letting go of these patterns, renews us and frees us to a world of endless possibilities and no expectations just the freedom to be our best self. This is our real self-renewed and enlightened, not bounded by the finite nature of whatever instant gratification our former obsessions or compulsions told us we needed to be happy. Not overwhelmed by the tragic nature, the ups and downs of this life and its empty promises.

Renewal of our minds and entrusting our life to the higher power overwhelms the finite and empowers us to see this life in its proper context, limited, flawed and at times enjoyable for the moment, but ultimately for what it is, finite. Nor is this an encouragement to drop out or check out. Beware! This is about taking back control of your own destiny in order to live a better life, your best life for you and others around you.

Let me give you an example of how this next passage from St Paul seemed to touch, stop and transform a life before my eyes.

"You must give up your old way of life; you must put aside your old self which gets corrupted by following illusory desires..."   *...Ephesians 4 v 22*

As a Prison Chaplain I met an interesting, even quirky, character that I met as part of the Prison Chaplaincy work. Mid 40's, pony tail, and to all intents and purposes, a new age traveller but not quite.

He came to the Chaplaincy over a completely different matter, and for once the Chaplaincy was fairly quiet which afforded us time to chat at length.

He seemed on the face of it quite confident, keen to disclose his past achievements, material achievements that is. In his home area he had built up a reputation as something of a pied piper. He was a landlord who had grown quite quickly and was well known as a provider to the social rent sector, to the point that those seeking affordable accommodation would follow him in the town and seek him out for available properties.

He chatted glowingly about his self-made success, the numbers of properties that he owned and, the extent of his own residential accommodation.

But then it came to the more personal issues of where it had all gone wrong and clearly, without too much disclosure, there were quality standards issues and also issues with inspection and revenue authorities.

As all of this unraveled, we came to chat about family. In the melee, there had clearly been some relationship problems, a separation and then suddenly the heart of it, the contact or lack of contact with his young son. There had been no barriers to contact placed by his partner, but clearly what became obvious was the pain caused by contact being limited to phone calls made from the prison corridor coin box.

Despite the detail about material gains and the property portfolio size, the one thing, the one unquantifiable commodity, the love of a father for his son was the one thing that brought this engaging, formerly buoyant, person to silence.

I happened to have on my desk and handed to him during this moment of silence, this passage from St Paul;

"You must give up your old way of life; you must put aside your old self which gets corrupted by following illusory desires..."   *...Ephesians 4 v 22*

Absolute silence as he read, re-read and came to terms with the meaning of the passage for his life. Tears wiped away and then; "Well yes, what can I say?"

Words, conversation, discussion between us thereafter were pointless. Somehow despite all the bravado and the talk of the quite obvious financial and social success, he had come face to face with his nemesis, the loss of meaningful contact with his son. Despite all of his success and notoriety, the mistakes that he had made left him powerless to keep contact with his son. He had come face to face with the root of his own emptiness, that the passing things of this life could never fill.

I did meet him in passing some short time later on one of the residential units and he said that he was busy making life plans and designing what he thought might be a quite innovative and successful website. It was or even is to be, a route-map for those seeking benefits and agencies for support. Intentionally though, and this he thought would be the innovative element of it, there would be parts of the website focusing on healthcare, lifestyles, exercise, diet and other welfare related aspects of life.

Not that the pied piper is alone amongst the prison population lured into first time and, for some, repeat offending by the promises of a materially focused life that we all lead.

At various times, many of us reach this point of powerlessness. Circumstances, people place us in a situation where without change we cannot move on. The need then is to move from powerlessness to change. The power to change is having hope. Power comes in the moment that you accept hope, hope to recover and reach the point of re-inventing yourself.

So the question for you in this Step 2 is whether you recognize that you have reached this point in your life? Have you discovered how powerless you are to control your life and, are you ready and able to surrender it in the hope of being transformed?

Hope is the power, the creative and loving energy that is always present, the power that each of us intuitively know that we are a part of. That each of us are invited to share in, unless we consciously reject it.

St Paul writes at length in many places about the power of hope, but most powerfully perhaps in his letter to the Romans.

"Now hope that is seen is not hope, for who hopes for what he sees? But if we hope for what we do not see, we wait for it with patience..."   *...Romans 8 v 24*

Patience, hope, trust, they all belong not to the addictions and short-lived fantasies of this world, but to something deeper within us that calls to the eternal, sacrificing the now for the hope of eternity.

What does psychologist Jordan Peterson mean by this? Sacrifice by its very nature does not just mean letting go of something, some way of being. There will be some pain in the process of sacrifice but it is a process and at the same time as letting go, it is conversely a taking back of our life and destiny and, the conscious step of choosing life over death, light over darkness, choosing the infinite over the finite.

It is the step that your best self, the inner voice within which knows intuitively this is the right and only step to take. Choose life. Choose the unseen.

St Paul writes:
"So we do not lose heart. Though our outer nature is wasting away, our inner nature is being renewed every day. For this slight momentary affliction is preparing us for an eternal weight of glory beyond all comparison, because we look not to the things that are seen but to the things that are unseen; for the things that are seen are transient, but the things that are unseen are eternal"   *... 2 Corinthians 4 v 16-18*

And that way is...   the way of love of life and of self.

Step 2: Hope

"Ultimate sacrifice, is the sacrifice of yourself to God" [4]

Step 3:

Make a decision to turn your will and your life over to God

> *"I can do all things with the help of the One who gives me strength ..."*
>
> ...*Philippians 4 v 13*

This will perhaps be the most difficult step to take as part of the transformation of your life.

Yes you have accepted that your life is beset by problems, problems that you have either allowed to overtake and possess you or those which you now realise have become your way of being with yourself and others.

But now having acknowledged that that there is a power greater than yourself, a power that is able to transform your life from its present powerless state of existence. Now you are called to act upon that acknowledgment.

A letter attributed to St James, the brother of the Lord, the author writes this:
> *"So faith by itself, if it has no works is dead"*...
>
> ...*James 2 v 17*

Acknowledgement of the higher power alone may not be sufficient to transform your life if you remain passive. You are also called to be an active participant and subsequently an ambassador for the power that exists to transform lives.

St Paul exhorts each of us to believe that anything is possible if we place our faith and hope in the one source who gives us strength.

In other words you have to become involved in the process to transform your life. You have already looked at your life, realised that there needs to be change, but that without a radical intervention and a new approach to your future, meaningful change is unlikely. That is either because you have tried many times before and failed or, because you and others around you know that you are otherwise powerless or reluctant to make the change necessary.

The mistake often made here is that people think, and honestly believe, that they can bring about change if they rely soley on their own will power. But you are dealing here with repetitive thinking, addictive behaviour and recurring patterns of behaving. These, by their very nature, imply that the chances of real change are limited if self-directed. You are called to action, but that must begin with the humility to accept that you need help too.

Now you are called to effect that change that will begin the process of transforming your life. A big step yes, but one you are now more confident of making with the support and power of the One who eternally loves you.

Perhaps here it may help to read the passage known to people of faith as the story of the "Prodigal Son".

"There was a man who had two sons. The younger of them said to his father, 'Father, give me the share of the property that will belong to me.' So he divided his property between them. A few days later the younger son gathered all he had and travelled to a distant country, and there he squandered his money on a life of debauchery.

When he had spent everything, a severe famine took place throughout that country, and he began to be in need. So he went and hired himself out to one of the citizens of that country, who sent him to his fields to feed the pigs. He would willingly have filled himself with the husks the pigs were eating but no one would let him have them.

But when he came to himself he said, 'How many of my father's hired hands have bread enough and to spare, but here I am dying of hunger! I will get up and go to my father, and I will say to him, "Father, I have sinned against heaven and before you; I am no longer worthy to be called your son; treat me like one of your hired hands."

So he set off and went to his father. But while he was still far off, his father saw him and was filled with compassion; he ran and put his arms around him and kissed him".

...Luke 15 v 11-20

Notice some of the descriptions used in the passage. The young man has exhausted all that the world has to offer, having travelled to a "distant land" in pursuit of his own ambition making the most of his inheritance, disregarding the will of his father and elder brother.

It is a "distant land" known by many with addictions to drugs or alcohol or, a distant land thrust upon those overcome by depression and anxiety, a distant land occupied at least for now by those overtaken by control issues.

Deep within each one who becomes lost in or, broken by this world, there is a voice, if they care to listen, a voice that they do recognise telling them not to go on living an aimless and broken life.

St Paul pleads with his community in Ephesus and with us here and now, to acknowledge and listen to that voice within. Transformation and new life begins with that moment of turning, of recognising a presence within. It is the light that comes with finding and accepting that presence, even in the midst of brokenness, that St Paul urges each of us to seek.

It can be found if you have the humility to accept that, for the moment at least, you are broken and beaten, but also that you need help if there is to be change.

Only you know how broken you feel, how powerless you are by yourself to do anything about it. Only you, and you alone, can make the decision to change Only you can decide to seek help from wherever it may come and then use that help to turn your life around from today, or whenever you decide, but preferably today.

Carpe diem!!! Seize the moment yes, have faith, but take it a moment at a time.

Step 3: Faith

"Set your sights at the Good, the Beautiful, and the True, and then focus pointedly and carefully on the concerns of each moment. Aim continually at Heaven while you work diligently on Earth. Attend fully to the future, in that manner, while attending fully to the present. Then you have the best chance of perfecting both" [5]

Step 4:

Make a searching and fearless review of yourself

"We ask God to fill you with Knowledge of His will, with all the wisdom and understanding that His Spirit gives..." Colossians 1 v 9B – 11

You have taken the courageous step to change, to hand over your past life in the hope of being transformed by and with the help of a power greater than yourself.

In a sense, you are naked before this power. Your flaws, your past mistakes, the wasteland of your former broken life lays exposed before you.

Accept this as a time of liberation, allow yourself the time and space simply to be. At this point you should not necessarily busy yourself with plans for the future making immediate commitments to prove to yourself and others your new found commitment to making a change.

This is partly a moment for reflection, to take stock and then to find out for yourself, and with the input of others if it helps, how your life has got to this place of brokenness. What has it been about your thinking patterns, the way that you have behaved, the ways that you have treated others and allowed your life to be over-powered and lost, that has brought you to this place of brokenness?.

It is a time, in other words, for being brutally honest without making excuses giving justifications or blaming others or circumstances of life. No, this is about you and is a time for taking ownership and responsibility for everything from your past up to the present.

St John writes this:

> *"If we cannot be condemned by our own conscience, we need have no fear in the presence of God"*   *...1 John 3 v 21*

So it is pretty clear that as brutal and as difficult as this process of taking ownership of your flaws may be, you need have no fear. That time of guilt, feeling powerless and beating yourself up has now passed.

You have acknowledged His presence and handed your life and well-being over to God or. St John and St Paul both speak with absolute confidence and reassurance that as you now turn back to God, invite His presence into your life and then trust your future into the power of His guidance, the past is already forgotten and all that exists is this moment and what is to be, it will be better.

This is a moment of great liberation as the weight of past failings and relapses is removed from your thinking and your mind.

The nature of life, of addictions, compulsions, obsessions and patterns of behaviour would easily and happily fill the void that you have allowed yourself, so there should also be a note of caution. It would be irresponsible and reckless, not also to be cautious if this time of liberation became itself a gateway back to a self-fulfilling loop of addictions and repeated patterns of behaviour.

In other words, perhaps this is a moment to create a list with a few simple headings look back on your past to ask who, why and how people many people you have hurt and in turn may have hurt you. Think about your own responsibility and also how you responded.

Have a read about this brief meeting with a prisoner on the day of his release, to see if there are any lessons to be learned for yourself as you too look forwards to your own future.

The Beach Man

As a Prison Chaplain I would meet during the last week of their confinement all those about to be released. The aim primarily was to ensure that they had a roof over their head on release, hopefully also some form of gainful employment and, to reflect for a few moments on the past mistakes and future plans.

So it was a surprise in early Spring to see a young man in his mid-20's and with some family commitments about to be released and, appearing in the Chaplaincy in a pair of shorts and a bright yellow T shirt, looking like the beach was the first stop upon release. The T shirt had a custom print photo of a Florida beach on the front.

"What is the plan on release?" "Two weeks rest at home, then I'm off to Florida with the kids for a month!" "And when you get back?" "No plans. Too soon. Just life" was the response that came my way. It was then on closer inspection of the T shirt, that I noticed these song lyrics printed round the edge of the photo of Florida. "Have you read what's on your T-shirt?" "What do you mean? What does it say?"

The song lyric that I knew well from George Harrison's last album;

"If you don't know where you're going, any road will take you there" was my reply. The lyrics read; *"Bow to God and call Him Sir, but if you don't know where you're going etc"* [6]

On release from prison, not knowing where you are going can quite often lead one back on the road to prison.

Drifting along the road of life may not be the best use of your time here and now and, and, may not be the best preparation for life hereafter if that indeed is what you might hope for. It may just seem co-incidental, almost not worth a second thought, but then how long does it take, how many opportunities have to present themselves to you before you relapse?

No you have to feel the benefit of your new found liberation, but at the same time, you have to take stock of the price that you and others have paid in reaching this point and then be sufficiently responsible and determined that you are not going back, asking God to grant you the benefit of His Spirit and wisdom helping you know the path that you should walk from hereon.

"Any Road" will not necessarily take you to the place that you want to be, the place that you deserve and were always meant to be.

"Try to realise it's all within yourself, no one can make you change
...but...life goes on within you and without you..." [7]

Life, this busy and sometimes chaotic life goes on around you. It quickly passes by, but now rather than drifting aimlessly in powerlessness, you can add meaning to your future by finding your own purpose in life and taking manageable steps to get there. It takes time and courage.

Step 4: Courage

"You must determine where you are going in your life, because you cannot get there unless you move in that direction. Random wandering will not move you forward. It will instead disappoint and frustrate you and, make you anxious and unhappy and hard to get along with (and then resentful, and then vengeful, and then worse)" [8]

Step 5:

Admit to God, to yourself, and to another person the exact nature of your wrongs.

"What we are is known to God, and I hope it is also known to your conscience..."
             ...2 Corinthians 5 v 11

These words of St Paul should not confront you, but what they are doing is asking you to bring to mind and account for mistakes that you have made, wrongs that you may have committed. They call you also to transformation. So here is the question that you need to ask yourself. How do you free yourself from your addiction, from your anxiety or whatever it is that is causing you to live in darkness?

The first step suggested by this process in day to day language I suppose is, to come clean. You cannot move on until you are absolutely honest with yourself about who or what you have become. The 12 Steps and St Paul are both recognising that this in any case is already known to God, but the healing and change begins when you admit this.

The problem is that you may think that you can deal with this entirely on your own. If you are absolutely honest with yourself, you may find that you have faced the question of how to free yourself many times before, and failed.

The failure lies not so much in your well-intentioned willingness to change, but rather in the very nature, flawed nature of your own make-up and, for that matter, all human make-up.

Remember at the beginning of these 12 Steps you were given this passage from St Paul to reflect upon:

"I cannot understand my own actions. For I do not do the good that I want, but the evil that I do not want, that is what I do..."   *... Romans 7 v 15-17*

Why is this the case? It is because you may genuinely believe that you can deal with your own flaws, addictions and life issues ourselves. You may not believe or see that you are a slave to your passions, needs, wants and your overall flawed nature.

Instead St Paul says that you need to attach ourselves to God by being honest, but this must be done in freedom and obedience. This should not be seen as surrendering one form of slavery for another, but rather the admission to God of the exact nature of your flaws, frees you from your past and opens the way for God's higher power to work in your life for your recovery and well-being; a freedom that you have not known, at least not of late.

You cannot be fully free if you do not fully unburden yourself from the past. Only you alone know how much there is to uncover and admit to, but experience shows that those who retain what is most hurtful or shameful to admit to, are the very ones most likely to relapse or fall back into old habits of behaving.

So this again is a step that is critical to your transformation and rebuilding. There can be no more self-deception, or being economic with the truth about yourself, otherwise you, or at least part of you, will remain isolated with your secrets, and never be fully free of them or your past. Complete transparency enables you to step away from who you are and have been towards the person that you want to be and can be. Possibly humiliating for you, but how liberating too?

St Paul recommends that you make the conscious decision to start afresh and not allow darkness or shadows of the past to rule in your life, but rather that to present yourself with all of flaws before God, the merciful and non-judgemental healer of your life. Unless you make this fearless admission, the grace of God cannot fully enter into and, transform your life.

This really is you recognising that something had to be done to change your life and then positively doing something about it, with the full knowledge and confidence that your acknowledgment and openness to God will be freely received without condemnation or condition. You can be sure that in God you have the perfect listener and giver of peace in return.

The next test of your newly found openness is you trying to find one other person whom you can be equally transparent and honest with. Ideally this would not be a close friend or relation but instead, someone whom you know to be a person of integrity and whose qualities you admire in terms of them being fair-minded, non-judgemental and, a good listener.

Humility is born out of this Step as you expose your flaws to someone that you trust.

What you don't need here is someone who may betray your trust as you share intimate details of your past. Nor can it be someone who may listen but then quickly form opinions about you and your real potential to change. You need a person of integrity to walk beside you.

The person that you choose should respect the path that you have chosen and be prepared to walk with you along these first few steps of new found hope.

Step 5: Integrity

"Act so that you do not become bitter and corrupt by the tragedy of existence
...confront the uncertainty of the world with faith and courage" 9

Step 6:

Be entirely ready for God to remove all defects of character.

"May you be strengthened in power through the Holy Spirit…so that Christ may dwell in your hearts and then planted on love and built on love you may have the strength to grasp the breadth and the length, the height and the depth and, to know the love of Christ which surpasses all knowledge …"

…Ephesians 3 v 16

This step now is one of consolidation at the same time as preparation and readiness for the journey ahead. It is also a step of healing as it calls for you to be ready for change.

Whilst you may think that you have achieved much since your first admission of powerlessness, personal transformation means that there is still much to do, and as important to be ready and prepared to do so.

This is no time for complacency, nor is it time for looking too far ahead. This step is about being in the moment and being open to the changes and challenges that inevitably lie ahead of you.

St Paul in this letter written for you, the Ephesians and countless generations since prays that the Holy Spirit will strengthen you, enlighten your mind and open your heart to the power of God that exists within you.

Step 6 encourages you to recognise the personal issues or defects that you may have and to be prepared to have these defects removed. In other words, this is yet another call to increase awareness of yourself, both in terms of what defects you have already addressed and those that remain to be considered in order that you may become the best person that you wish to be.

You are already aware of the power of God to bring about change and transformation. Now the characteristics of that transformation and the increasing awareness of a spiritual presence within your very self, is a resource for you to draw upon.

St Paul recognises that that power, namely the love of God within, can achieve so much more than we can ask or imagine. He talks of it as if we have to try in any way humanly possible to understand the height and depth, length and breadth of God's love moving within us; a boundless, immeasurable, non-judgemental and eternal love.

It is a process of allowing yourself to be utterly receptive to renewal and transformed in the way that you live your life, being prepared to allow your life to be guided, not by your own wants and needs, nor by your previous obsessions and patterns of living. Instead now the foundation for your way of living is love itself; love of yourself, of and love for others.

In this way, and with love as a foundation for all of your thoughts and actions, the power of God brings new hope and meaning to your life and the lives of others with whom you live, work and enjoy time with. They too become aware of and benefit from this transformation in your life.

This is why St Paul writes about the power of God being able to achieve more than we can ask or imagine.

In your previous state of powerlessness, you may hardly have ever considered that your life and way of living was of any value to yourself, let alone the being able to bring value to the lives of others that have had to support you or, at best, to tolerate the ways you were with them.

Now it could be your own renewed life that has the power to transform the lives of others.

Step 6 then on this pathway to new life calls for you to be ready, willing and able to acknowledge and accept the power of God to change all aspects of your life and the way that you live it.

Step 6: Willingness

"What shall I do when I am tired and impatient"...Gratefully accept an outstretched hand" [10]

Step 7:

Humbly ask God to remove your shortcomings

"We have this treasure in earthen vessels to show that the power belongs to God and not to us ..."　　　　　　　　　　　　　　　...2 *Corinthians 4 v 7*

In the days that St Paul wrote this letter to his community in Corinth, earthen vessels (pot jars) were often used to carry fine oils or wine; simple everyday pots carrying something of great worth.

So what does this passage mean as far as your journey of transformation is concerned and how, if at all, does it apply to you and your circumstances?

You, we, each of us are the earthenware made by the hands and love of our Creator, your higher power. As with any hand-made pot we each come with our own flaws and imperfections. You may have considered, may still consider but hopefully not for long at this stage, that you are too imperfect, have too many issues, have caused too much harm or damage to others, to be of any value to anyone.

The letting go of your powerlessness and handing over of your future to a higher power, THE higher power of God, should by now have convinced you that this is not the case and that change is possible.

It does not matter how difficult it is to prove your worth and your willingness to change in the eyes of other people, even members of your own family whom you think may have given up on you.

God, your creator, never gives up on you, never could give up on you. God is always in the background waiting, hoping that you will repent and turn to Him. But you should also know and believe that you are forgiven and healed at the moment of turning, of handing over your life to His care.

This is the reassurance that you need when so many backs have been turned on you, when you have received too many rejections and failed too many times.

This is truly humbling when you learn and actually begin to accept that you are, you have been and always will be truly loved and forgiven.

True humility is the lesson to be learned in this step, when as St Paul writes, we accept that the power belongs to God and not to us. Humility in this sense is not accepting how worthless you are, but is realising and fully accepting your own real worth. This should not just give you the confidence boost that you have so longed for, but should also encourage you to look to the future and what it may hold for you.

As insignificant as you may have felt in the greater scheme of things, God can use you with all of your flaws and imperfections.

Not only can you be healed and your life along with that of others changed, but you, your story, your transformation may be the spark that others need to be able to see in order to change their own chaotic lives.

This is true humility when you can accept that you can be an instrument of change for others by the power of the One who made you.

Step 7: Humility

"You must decide whether you want to be right or you want to have peace. You must decide whether to insist on the absolute correctness of your view, or to listen and negotiate. You don't get peace by being right" [11]

Step 8:

Make a list of people harmed and be willing to make amends.

"Let go of all bitterness, passion and anger; no more shouting or insults; no more hurtful feelings of any kinds. Instead, be kind and tender hearted, forgiving one another..."

...Ephesians 4 v 31

This passage from St Paul begins with possibly the most difficult words and process that you have had to face on your own personal journey. Words that you might never have considered possible before the process began.

Letting go does not come naturally for someone who has little control over their own life, nor does it come any more easily for the person whose control and addictive traits have impacted and curtailed the lives of others including family, friends and colleagues.

Bitterness, passion and anger are deep-seated emotions and they will not only have affected the way you think about yourself and others, but they will have caused others to have formed opinions based on the way you have behaved or spoken to them. These may be fairly fixed ideas about yourself and how they perceive you.

Step 8 then turns attention from yourself to towards the people that you may have willingly or inadvertently harmed. So whilst this is a pretty difficult step to take, it is also fundamental if the life of yourself and others is to change for the better.

Nevertheless it does still involve yourself. St Paul writes about letting go of bitterness, passion and anger. Each of these in different ways and at different times will have distorted the way that you have looked at yourself or the world around you.

Whilst it all depends on the circumstances you may bear some or all of the responsibility, but nevertheless now is the time to forgive yourself and, make amends to others. It all begins with you. It has to. This is not being self-centred or selfish. The change has to begin with you as no-one else can change the way you think, behave or see the world.

Next, and again it very much depends on the circumstances, there may be people in your day to day life who have to deal with you and your former self. Only you will know who they are, how difficult it may have been for them, how they may have been affected or how they may have been hurt by yourself. Only you and they know how much they have been prepared or had to put up with because of their love, duty and care for you.

At the same time you may have become hurt or resentful towards them because at various times they actually may have found it difficult to support and encourage you in the way that you felt was necessary. For example someone in the middle of sudden panic attacks or acute health anxieties either may not be reassured by the words of support offered by another or, may think they just don't take your genuine concerns about your health seriously enough. Yet you cannot blame others for your behaviour towards them no matter how insensitive they may appear to have been.

So much may have happened and so much hurt may been caused and yet St Paul reminds us that it is absolutely necessary and right to let go and not to hold onto any hurtful feelings towards one another.

Not only is it necessary and right for them, but also if you are to truly transform your life, how can you move on unless you are prepared to be brutally honest with yourself and accept the harm that you have done, and how can you prevent further negative thoughts about others from continuing to cause damage to your own well-being and that of others.

Whilst all of these failures of yours may be difficult to list and therefore make amends to people for, there may be others, possibly countless others, who have been adversely affected or hurt by you and the unintended consequences of your thoughts, words or actions. These too should at least be considered by you and named as far as you are able to.

The end result will be a list, yes possibly an embarrassing list, but it should at the end of the process give you a clear conscience and, a sense of being at peace with yourself and others. St Paul encourages this as being a way of putting things right between yourself and the world around you. It is also a spiritual way of living with others. You cannot expect forgiveness, if you yourself are not willing to forgive.

Anything less than this seemingly brutal process of being honest can risk further damage to yourself and your chance of making a full recovery.

The Bin Man

A prisoner comes to mind, who whilst on holiday with his friends, received a phone call from his sister to say that his partner of 10 years, was cheating on him whilst he was absent.

He promptly caught a plane home, threw a bin through the front window of his own house and after climbing in severely beat both partner and friend. He received 7 years imprisonment in consequence.

When we met some three years after conviction, he was still extremely angry behaving in a volatile manner and, at risk of prolonged imprisonment. After several hours over several days of listening, the question was why was he still allowing her to hurt him and jeopardise his future?

Time, tears and some amount of reflection allowed him to review and to make a new resolve to move on.

What lessons can we learn from this? As a passive observer perhaps it was too simplistic for me, the chaplain, to look at the situation described with such passion, and then to offer advice on alternative ways of responding.

In the heat of the moment and an emotionally charged situation, a young man still in love with a woman he had known since his youth, had responded affirmatively but aggressively to a provocative but also demeaning situation. He had been cheated on by someone that he loved and built a life around.

But even months after the event, the bitterness, resentment and anger still ate away at him with damaging implications for his future and his psychological well-being.

St Paul may well write; *"Let go of all bitterness, passion and anger. No more hurtful feelings of any kind..." ...Ephesians 4 v 31*, but here a life, a future had been ripped apart by human weakness.

Evil operates at this level. It sees our weaknesses. It exposes our vulnerabilities. It exploits our tendencies.

Not only does it exploit, but it continues to feed and drive our human desire for retaliation and revenge. Bitterness, passion and anger are the very tools that it needs to expose our vulnerabilities. Add in self-pity and low self-esteem and, you have a toxic mix explosive enough to ignite and re-ignite retaliation and revenge.

And round and round it goes in a downward spiral unless somehow we, or we with the help of others, are able to arrest it, put it into the perspective of life as a whole and, find the capacity within to rebuild, if not the distance at first to forgive.

It is all scriptural

We have to acknowledge our human weakness, to come to terms with the real existence of evil, to understand its causes and impacts but then, to be able to reach out, regain our equilibrium and rebuild our lives with a renewed perspective. We have to somehow search for the light and turn our back on the shadows of darkness.

Don't look back in anger!

Bitterness, passion and anger are extremes and may, at the time, appear to be a valid response to hurt caused by another. It is holding onto the hurt that is damaging, both for yourself and others.

People, situations, disappointments, hurt us and it is not at all easy but for our emotional, physical and spiritual welfare, sometimes we can do no more than to let go and look only to the future. Reparation where possible is the key.

Bitterness, passion and anger cannot undo the past, but they can undo the future.

Step 8: Reparation

"Make friends with people who want the best for you" [12]

Step 9:

Make direct amends to others wherever possible, except when to do so would injure them or others.

"If possible, so far as it depends on you, be at peace with one another..."

...Romans 12 v 18

Both the 12 Steps Big Book and St Paul encourage living peacefully and making amends but also add a note of caution to any action that you might wish to take in making reparation to others for past behaviour.

Making reparation and amends is a necessary step not only in terms of accepting your own failures but also, in accepting the harm that these failures may have caused. It is also necessary in enabling you to move forwards whilst acknowledging the harm caused.

"So far as it depends on you". It is you, your words, behaviour or lack of care for others that has caused the harm. You have already accepted that as part of the recovery process, and all of this is positive, self-motivated and absolutely worthwhile. You should be in no doubt about this whatever happens next.

What you cannot guarantee or control is how other people will respond, whether they will accept that you have changed and forgive you or, not be able to trust your resolve or genuine contrition.

It may be that they have been hurt too much to forgive you at least at the moment or, that the damage caused to the relationship, themselves or family is just too substantial in their eyes.

Only you know how genuinely sorry you are. Likewise, only others know how much hurt you have caused them. It's a fact and the sooner that you realise and accept that, the better placed you will be to understand your relationship towards others now.

Their acknowledgement of your apology is beyond your control and has to be accepted without resentment, otherwise it risks further impact on yourself or harm to others.

However, the guidance for this step cautions against making amends if to do so would cause further harm. This is very much down to individual circumstances. Only you will know the answer to this. It is a question of judgement, but even if the conclusion is reached that it would be better not to make the approach, it should not undermine your own transformation. Rather see this as further evidence of your own personal growth and responsibility. This is now you taking into account the feelings and circumstances of others. This is progress. This is spiritual growth.

When have you been able to consider others recently? Previously the feelings of others might not have had any impact on you. Now you are able to care.

Whilst to make amends and seek forgiveness would have been your preference, you are now able to acknowledge and accept the harm that you have caused, but still be at peace with the fact that another individual does not accept your remorse, for the time being at least.

In his letter to the Romans, St Paul encourages members of the community to "do what is right in the eyes of everyone. If possible, so far as it depends on you, be at peace with one another" This was good practical advice when it was written and, it still holds true today. You simply have to be realistic in your expectations of others, you cannot control how they will respond and behave towards you.

Not only is this practical advice, it is the spiritual path that you, we all are being guided along by the letters of St Paul. The call is where possible to be peacemakers, not to repay evil with evil but rather to hold fast to what is good.

It can take time to recognise the place that we need to be between good and evil but by taking these practical steps to transform your life, you are taking the path towards a better and positive way of living.

One final thought regarding this step. Whenever possible, and again not being harmful to others, it is better to make your apology and put things right by taking a personal approach. This is about you accepting responsibility, showing humility and your genuine desire to be a peacemaker.

A personal approach may not always possible, but bear in mind that texts and phone calls can be misinterpreted by the receiver and risk further harm if the right words are not chosen.

Sometimes the physical act of sitting down and writing a heartfelt letter of apology is good practice. It disciplines you and really makes you think carefully about what you want and must say. It also gives the person receiving it something tangible to hold onto and may help them to understand and accept that there is genuine remorse about what has happened.

Let me give you an example where a well-written letter led to healing for both parties involved, one a prisoner I had the privilege to meet. The other a teacher that I didn't have the opportunity to meet personally.

John, I first met in 2014 when he was in his early 20's. Immediately engaging and with a magnetic personality that I couldn't help but be drawn to as deep down there was a sense that this was a thoroughly good person with so much potential to offer.

Not someone with a faith that was practiced at least, but someone whom you could see had the potential to lead a decent, fulfilled life. He described himself as having always been a "grafter". Out of necessity and to help himself, he had since the age of 13 always sought opportunities to earn money, to earn his keep as his one parent family struggled to make ends meet in inner city Manchester.

From that age he had cycled at weekends into Manchester to work on the markets from 4.00am in the morning.

By his own admission, he was a poor student with little interest, no parental boundaries and, sensing that he was in a constant struggle to make his mark in life.

This resulted in ongoing clashes with school authorities which ultimately imploded when challenged by one of his teachers he lashed out, assaulted the teacher and was immediately and permanently excluded from education at the age of sixteen.

At risk then and because of the inner city culture and company that he kept, driven by his "grafter" nature to succeed, he was drawn into the underworld of drugs, not as a user, but as a supplier.

His nature was such that he quickly progressed developing networks, meeting and surviving many physical risks to become what some might nowadays call a cross county lines supplier.

Ultimately, due to intelligence, infiltration and mobile phone surveillance he was detected, arrested and imprisoned for conspiracy with others to supply class "A" drugs and given an initial 5 year sentence which was due to end in September 2014.

Though not a young man with faith, we would spend time in the Chaplaincy over a cup of coffee, exploring his background and seeking ways to transform this driven life in order that he could succeed in a restored and resettled lifestyle.

The glimmer of hope that I had was his own admission that the "bad money" that he had earned or come about through drugs had "never lasted". It came, he said, from "a bad place" where suffering in South America linked to the drugs trade was commonplace. It brought with it rewards and misery in equal measure.

Whilst he enjoyed the trappings of its rewards because of its potential and meaning for his life, he closed his mind to the misery that its supply to others would inflict.

So, how to break this cycle and what hope might there be to restore the potential that this thinking, grafting life offered?

St Paul writes; "*do not be conformed to the pattern of this world, but be transformed by the renewal of your mind*"....Romans 12 v 12

What would be the best way to transform and renew the mind this young man with potentially so much goodness in him and so much to offer life, yet constantly drawn by this life to the darker side of human weakness?.

Occasional, informal chats continued as the time for his release approached and then what appeared to be the breakthrough that might transform his life. It was a breakthrough of his own making and it was responded to.

Some 10 years had passed since the assault that caused his exclusion from school. Because of the immediate exclusion he had never since seen his victim, the teacher in question, or had an opportunity to apologise.

He had decided that now, before his release, was the time for a long overdue apology. He wanted some help to write a sincere letter just to place on record his sorrow for what had happened, but also his acknowledgement of the longer lasting and undeserved hurt that an incident such as this might cause in the mind and to the confidence of an individual whose profession was there to serve and improve the life chances of those in their care.

The guidance for Step 9 cautions against making amends or attempting to do so if to do so would cause further harm.

And so, some sensitive enquiries were made by myself with the school, firstly to establish whether the teacher might still be a staff member, but also to enquire whether they might be receptive to this, unsolicited but genuine, approach. They were and a letter was duly written and, in due course, responded to.

Healing took place and hope was restored for both parties. By the time the response was received, J had been released, but in a sense that point seemed to matter less, as closure had been reached, two lives had been restored and, in one life at least there was hope for a more positive lifestyle.

The reply from the teacher, when it was received, was one of heartfelt gratitude but also of hope for a more positive outcome for all the past investment in the life of one of their pupils.

The hope was that a mind had been renewed and that conformity with the patterns and darkness of this world had been broken.

St Paul constantly reminds us to be on our guard as evil and darkness exist to draw us from the light and from hope. He urges us to act "becomingly as in the day" and not to allow darkness to overcome us as in the night.

Recognise that making amends restores justice and shows a commitment to the continuous process of change?

Making amends will ultimately realign your thinking and over time, you will inwardly know it was the right and only thing to do.

Step 9: Justice

"What have I done wrong and what can I do now to make things a little better?" [13]

Step 10:

Monitor yourself and take responsibility

"Brothers you were called and chosen as you know to liberty; be careful as this liberty will provide an opportunity for indulgence..."   *...Galatians 5 v 13-14*

This advice from St Paul is asking you to be careful. Liberty for you is a state that has been hard won and only you may know how easy it would be to fall back into the way of living that would render you powerless and lose control of your life for a while.

There is a fine line to tread and keeping that state of equilibrium will be a constant process of monitoring yourself, your thoughts, your emotions, your actions and, your relationships to make sure that your path stays focussed on the person, the person that you want to be, the you that you have rediscovered and were always meant to be.

In a way it sounds that it may be tiresome and a challenge but life is just that for everyone, a constant series of challenges and choices. St Paul recognises and, you yourself have come to know, that the nature of yourself and everyone is that we are all prone to failure. But neither should this timely advice fill you with fear of the day to day or indeed of the future.

So how do you go about monitoring yourself and acting on this advice? From now on it is about restoring meaning to your life or, perhaps giving it a meaning that it had previously lacked or lost.

This step is really about self-awareness. You need to learn here how to watch your habits, your patterns of thinking and acting. It's easier than you might think once you get into the habit of monitoring. Remember, you have developed habits before, just maybe not the right ones for your life.

This is about you accepting responsibility for your life and placing a value on yourself and your life.

Value in any sense of the word implies that there is a cost involved and a cost likewise implies giving something up. This in turn means risk uncertainty and possible reward.

Be careful with the reward because you know too well the price that you have paid, the cost to yourself and others when your focus was firmly fixed on the reward rather than the way of getting there, on instant gratification in the moment rather than reward and meaning in the future.

"Proper being is a process not a destination" [14]

Peterson is saying exactly that, that in order to take responsibility for your own life and monitor progress, you should set yourself achievable goals. It is a process of taking small steps, realising that one by one you are achieving them and, gaining confidence in your own ability, improving your self-worth and ultimately giving value and meaning to your life.

As you look back at what you have achieved from now on you may be able to say to yourself that it wasn't easy but that it was worth it. In fact if you have reached this step in the process of rebuilding your life and regaining your liberty, then you have already achieved and restored some meaning.

St Paul reminds us that this is not to say that life from now on will be easy. It's a process and there will be risk, there will be challenges, but it is in facing those challenges that you will give meaning to your life.

Confronting the challenges allows you to learn about yourself, makes you learn who you can be. Deeper within yourself now you are coming to re-discover and know yourself again. You are listening to the Spirit within, being guided and accepting responsibility for your own future.

All the while it is a day by day, achievement by achievement process. In this way it is a process of constant growth but at the same time remaining clearly focussed on the moment. Accept happiness and be grateful for what you are achieving but realise also that happiness itself is in the moment and, that it is not a goal that you should set yourself.

Taking responsibility now means creating a strategy, a series of manageable steps setting out what you would like to achieve, monitoring yourself as you take some steps, possibly and probably faltering steps at first, but steps nevertheless.

The steps should stretch you and test your new self-confidence, but also they should not be immediate or for the purpose of instant self-gratification. This type of quick fix for happiness may be one of the reasons that you became lost or broken in the first place.

It is a question of living responsibly, aiming for what is in the long term interest of yourself and others around you. In this way you will be safeguarding your own liberty and serving the higher purpose that you have now come to recognise.

St Paul explains it in these words:

> "*If we live by the Spirit, we should also try to walk by the Spirit*"
>
> *...Galatians 5 v 12*

But phrases such as "living by the Spirit" and "walking by the Spirit" may sound like alien phrases especially if you have not previously had any kind of faith.

So how is it best to explain this? You have come to the conclusion that your life is out of control, you need to change and have decided to do so. This advice from St Paul then can be read as how to go about changing. In other words, the qualities in your behaviour that will allow yourself and others to see the changes in your behaviour. It's about showing care for others, consideration and kindness, listening and looking out for others in your daily life.

It may only be as you look back that the results of your decision to change become clear. In that time frame others may come to notice a real change in you. Whilst they may not explain it as St Paul does, what they are actually seeing in you are the very same spiritual qualities that St Paul encourages you to adopt as the hallmark of your life and your way of living.

This is "walking by the Spirit" and successfully taking Step 10 of the process. In other words, actively allow God to show you the path that you should take. Persevere and all will be well.

Step 10: Perseverance

"Proper being is a process not a destination" [15]

Step 11:

Seek through prayer and meditation to improve conscious contact with God praying only for knowledge of His will for you

"You must live your whole lives according to the Christ you have received; you must be rooted in Him and built on Him and, held firm by the faith you have been taught..."

...Colossians 2 v 6

Some people talk of our powerlessness before God and they are of course referring to the omnipotence of God, a God who knows, sees, endures and, enables all things. Yes endures, because we humans, all of us, walk away from at some point or, actively avoid any reliance upon the power of God, the grace and enduring love that God has for each of us.

Strangely it is your own powerlessness in the face of a chaotic lifestyle that has brought you to this place of surrender before the power of God. But in equal measure this step encourages you to be at peace from the chaos, in trust and reliance upon the mercy, forgiveness and power of God.

St Paul writes about being rooted in Christ and Christ himself said...*for apart from me you can do nothing ...John 15 v 5*

Do not be misled into thinking that you are surrendering one form of powerlessness and lack of control for another by trusting God and allowing Him to take control of your life.

This form of dependence is entirely different like nothing you could ever have known or encountered in your previous life. This is attaching yourself to a life-giving tree, grafting yourself onto what Christ refers to as the true vine.

But as a branch you have to be nurtured and from time to time pruned. Nurtured by constant prayer and pruned in the sense that you have to now be open and honest before God. Allow your flaws to be exposed. Remember as we have said previously God can use your weakness for His purpose as well as, and sometimes in spite of, your strengths.

True nurturing comes from communication with God. How can you know His purpose for your life if you do not engage in conversation with or allow Him to speak to you?

Prayer is the key to good communication. As St Paul writes.....
"pray constantly that you may know the will of God for your life..."

...1 Thessalonians 5 v 17

By prayer he does not mean the constant repetition of prayers learned in your childhood or along the way. No prayer in this sense is simply bringing yourself and your being into the presence of God both to listen and guide you. You may come to a place of stillness within by perseverance.

In His teaching Christ said; *"when you pray take yourself off into your private place and pray before your Father and your Father who sees all that is done in private will reward you" ... Matthew 6 v6*

It is perhaps something that you have not been used to for some time, if ever. No matter, this is a step encouraging you to be at one with God and allowing Him to guide you. It is about holding nothing back, but instead being open and transparent with a power that loves you unconditionally, that wants only good for you, for you to live your best life. Enter into the process and over time and again with perseverance, it may bring you a peace the like of which you have never known, far removed from your previous life of chaos.

This is taking step 11 to heart and committing yourself to improving and maintaining your contact with and trust in God, a God who has you in His keep that you need have no fear for the future, because He sees it and He wills a better life for you.

Seek and find it through prayer, spirituality and quiet contemplation of the real Presence in your life.

Step 11: Spirituality

"Aim for wisdom...distil that wisdom into words and speak forth those words as if they matter, with true concern and care".[16]

Step 12:

After your own spiritual awakening, convey the message to others.

"God helps us in all our troubles, so that we are able to help others in any kind of trouble with the same help that we ourselves have been given ..."

...2 Corinthians 1 v 4

There are different ways of looking at this the twelfth and final step that you take.

Firstly, St Paul is asking you to consider two things. He says that there is a merciful God, your Creator, who might at times seem remote and therefore irrelevant to your day to day living, but who nevertheless is constantly present and wills that you turn to Him for help and guidance.

Secondly, you have now taken the previous steps and acknowledge the presence of God. St Paul reminds you to be thankful for the help that you have received to transform a life that seemed to be in chaos.

Being thankful also serves to reaffirm the transformation that has taken place in your life. As you look back, you can now see the change that has taken place and looking at the change you recognise that though it wasn't easy, it was worth it in terms of the personal growth that has taken place.

As a result of your own self-belief, your own efforts and the trust that you have placed in the spiritual journey, you are now both physically and psychologically in a better place and also more enlightened as to the power that can be called upon to help you.

This spiritual journey that you have been on now calls on you to be an ambassador for change in the lives of others. You have received help in the first faltering steps that you took to transform your life and that responsibility falls to you to seek to help others in their first steps. The challenge to take the message to others is a means to serve a higher purpose than just helping yourself.

This is not payback and it should not be seen as some onerous task that is expected of you in return for the help that you have received. Rather, see this as a privilege and a trust that has been given to you. There is an opportunity now to try and help other travellers on the road to transformation.

It is not so much a duty as an affirmation of your own change that you are now better equipped to help others with the same help that you yourself received. In other words, you are now called to be selfless, another final step in your own growth.

This step, if you embrace it, will also help you further in gaining a sense of purpose for your own life. Not that this should just be for personal reward, but the satisfaction of enabling others to see their own seemingly hopeless place reaffirms your transformation. You are now an ambassador for the possibility of recovery and transformation. You and your journey will be able to guide the first tentative steps of others.

Care, compassion and kindness are all spiritual gifts that can bring blessings and hope to the lives of others. Who better to bring these blessings and support than yourself who has lived the experience of powerlessness and suffering that can envelop a life. Others will more readily listen to you because you have lived their experience and understand their brokenness.

Little did you know, could you have known, in the midst of your own suffering that one day you might just be the inspiration, the hope and the servant that others needed to inspire them.

As you step back to realise this, you may start to consider that this was all part of a bigger plan that you too have been trusted to be part of.

Step 12: Service

" Extend the hand of trust to someone that his or her best part can step forward to reciprocate..."[17]

Conclusion:

"If the Spirit doesn't move you, what's the use of making plans?" [18]

What to write in a conclusion that has not already been written?

Firstly. The 12 Steps should be acknowledged. It is well known that since they were introduced by Alcoholics Anonymous back in the 1950's, the 12 Steps have provided a foundation and a process for the healing and recovery of millions who have committed to them.

The first point to underline in the conclusion then, as has been said throughout, is that the 12 Steps in whatever format they are presented, require commitment.

The fact that there are 12 Steps itself shows that the 12 Steps are a process and not a quick fix.

Nor are the Steps some form of Pick'n Mix, where you can drop in, try the ones that appeal to you and avoid those that either don't fit with your lifestyle or the way that you think about your life.

What is also true is that the 12 Steps have since their publication been adapted for a whole range of addictions, personal flaws and behaviours.

In other words, they are a trusted process. They can work for you, if you trust them, and entrust yourself to them.

So you have to know that if the challenge that you face is an addiction, there is a way out; if it is depression or an anxiety issue, there is a way back; if it is separation, divorce or, grief after loss, there is a way forward.

The key to each of these is hope. You have to have, or at least believe that you can rediscover, hope. Hope provides you with the first tiny steps that, when taken, give you the confidence and self-belief to take more.

Again this is a process, and so the steps also demand some level of patience, a patience that will bear fruit as you recover your self-belief and self-esteem.

As if to sum up the personal requirements of the process, St Paul writes this;

"We rejoice in our sufferings knowing that sufferings produce endurance, and endurance produces character, and character produces hope and, hope does not disappoint us....."
...Romans 5 v 3

St Paul is being honest with his readers. Even though people may hold onto a faith, it does not mean that life will be without its challenges. That is the nature of life for all. But he argues that for people of faith, there is the reassurance of hope in a God who loves all and, ultimately a God who will give a peace beyond the knowledge or wherewithal of this world.

So this then is the final step. In addition to commitment, patience, endurance and hope, can you in your place of brokenness reach out into the depths and place your trust in the spiritual world and, the caring eternal power of a God who loves you? This too takes time, commitment, trust and hope.

For me personally, the writings and guidance of St Paul have time and again provided me with the reassurance and encouragement to move forward.

For you it may be different, but the Scriptures as a whole are there for you to sit with, read and allow the Word of God to reveal itself to you, providing you with a path which you could choose to follow.

The only caution that I would add, as is the case for each of the 12 Steps, is not to make the mistake of thinking that you know all the answers, but rather to be open to following the signs that may be placed in your path to help you.

Let me give you an example of one such sign, which at the time I either did not recognise or, in my foolishness or weakness (call it what you will), chose not to follow and subsequently realised that I should have.

∞   ∞   ∞   ∞

Should I stay or should I go?...a Sign missed...a Lesson in Trust!

My first Chaplaincy experience was at HMP Lancaster Castle, an ancient and seemingly austere even hostile environment which itself had seen so many battles and trials in its almost 1000 year history but there was a sense also there that, not just the Chaplaincy, but the various other departments within the prison were all part of a battle of steadfastness but also of restoration for those in their care. It was a team effort, a caring team at that.

But then in 2011 a change of Government, public sector cuts and what appeared to be a knee-jerk decision to close HMP Lancaster Castle by the then Home Secretary, shocked not only staff but inmates also.

There followed a relatively brief and almost callous rolling programme of closure with inmates being "decanted" to a number of regional prisons and staff being subject to a process the MOJ refer to as "mapping" which is HR terminology for re-allocating resources to other prison establishments, taking into account where possible staff travel distances so as to minimise travel claims.

For me as chaplain this entailed a move to another Chaplaincy team at a young offenders' prison across the city, namely HMP Lancaster Farms.

The beating heart and shining soul of the HMP Lancaster Castle Chaplaincy team, Carolyn, had perhaps seen the writing on the wall and heeded the rumours by retiring some three months prior to the announcement. She had been replaced, somehow without open recruitment, by someone I would describe as a pen pusher with little interest or commitment to those in our care, whose greatest aspiration appeared to be for self-promotion and personal advancement.

In some senses then, Carolyn having left, this closure appeared to be timely and another lesson learned over the years, as to how light and darkness can never co-exist.

The closure came and went and, the transfer itself came and then went. At a time like this the MOJ will give a period of grace for the move, re-adjustment and will include an option to terminate your own employment within a given period.

Whilst to be kind, the new Chaplaincy team were efficient and statutory duties compliant, the heart, the commitment and the passion seemed less evident.

This, of course, is subjective but whereas at the Castle the Spirit was moving, the spirit at the young offenders' prison was, well, business like. The environment of the prison itself was chaotic, constantly charged by outbreaks of violence and alarm bells ringing as youngsters let off steam.

The deadline set for the period of grace given by the MOJ loomed with "should I stay, should I go?" see sawing in my brain. My spirit wanted to follow one path, but my mind and every sinew screamed again; "Go while you have chance!".

By the Tuesday before the weekend deadline for decisions, and in sheer panic mode, I firstly sought a meeting with the Chaplaincy Manager who, to be fair, was very supportive and encouraging stating that should I leave it would mean "the loss of a gifted chaplaincy member".

I decided to stay late that evening and take refuge in the Chapel to pray and seek some kind of guidance. To be honest that was not my normal way of decision making.

This feeling of being torn between heart and mind never happened to me before, and looking back it is so obvious and yet so damning of my own flawed human nature, but then what does St Paul write?

"I cannot understand my own actions. The thing I most want to do, I never do and yet, the thing that I least want to do, that is what I do..."   *...Romans 7 v 15-17*

So I was alone in a secure chapel. I sit and my mind is doing cartwheels back and forth between stay and go. Prayer and mindfulness at that point was a non-starter for me. I decided to pick up the nearest bible, open it and read the first paragraph of whatever lay before me as I opened it.

This is what I read;

"But how are they to call on Him, if they do not believe in Him; and how will they believe if they have not heard; and how will they hear unless there is a preacher; and how will there be a preacher unless one is sent?"

... Romans 10 v 14

As chaotic as it was, the inmates at Lancaster Farms were no less deserving of someone, no matter how weak, to guide them than those at the Castle had been. The option to choose was obvious.

So why after several further days of inner wrangling did I opt to resign? Self-preservation, weakness, lack of trust, loss? All of these come to mind and that, as they say, might have been that.

A much wiser, more spiritual, pastoral guide sat with me early on the

Monday morning after I had submitted the letter to the MOJ the previous Saturday morning. He urged me to make an immediate call to the MOJ HR department and rescind the resignation. The letter had just been received by the HR department, but it was determined by the HR team to be final and irreversible.

At that point, I was a former prison chaplain but Fr Chris sitting with me simply said; "Don't think young man that if God wants you as a prison chaplain, He won't be able to get you back in!" A lesson in trust, of which I had none.

A Lesson:

At times in all of our lives, we are faced with what appear to be impossible choices. They can be made, although in my case not that well at a human, rational, emotional level. But we can and maybe should, if we are people of faith, even of little faith, be humble, acknowledge our weakness, seek spiritual guidance, listen...and then follow whatever we sense within to be the right course.

St Paul wrote;

> *"pray constantly, giving thanks to God in all circumstances"*
>
> *... 1 Thessalonians 5 v 17*

But then there is another step, another lesson to learn beyond humility and prayer. It is the lesson of trust.

We have to trust that we can be guided by the Spirit, by a higher power if that is your preference. Trust that we will be guided to make a choice that will be for good, even if at the time it may not appear to be good for ourselves.

We also have to be aware that our humanity, our brokenness and weakness will immediately kick in and offer us so many reasons why we should not listen to that inner voice.

For me, I can only say that the recognition of my own weakness and, my regret that I had not followed the guidance printed in front of my eyes, was followed literally by months of mourning for a lost opportunity, sorrow and apology for lives that I might have been able to touch. There followed a search in the darkness, or so it seemed, for a moment to make amends.

The lessons then.
Pray, search, listen, respond, but above all else, read the signs and trust.

I genuinely hope that you will be given signs that will lead you towards the light or a better place than you presently may be at. I believe that the letters of St Paul might help you. I know that the 12 Steps themselves are a tried and tested route map to transformation and healing.

I trust that God will renew your mind and, reveal his plans for your life.
I wish you health, recovery and, happiness.

Appendix:

Knowing You...some questions to help you

1. Your background.
    - What do you think has most shaped your life?
    - What are/were your relationships like with your parent(s), family, friends?
    - Have you ever felt like you didn't matter in your family, at work, in your close relationships?
    - Have you ever had a feeling of being bullied, threatened, rejected, or blamed unfairly?

2. Your fears.
    - Do you worry about what other people might think or feel about you?
    - Do you sense that people think that you are bad, disgusted by you?
    - Do you feel rejected or fear being harmed by others?
    - Do you feel or see yourself as unworthy?
    - Do you fear that you can't cope, or that you are always angry and at risk of losing control?
    - What are you most afraid of?

3. Your safety.
    - What do you do to cope when you fear something?
    - How do you face your fears?
    - What do you do to protect yourself from other people?.
    - What do you do to protect yourself from your own thoughts, feelings, and memories?

4.   Your actions and their consequences.

- Do you ever think about the possible undesirable consequences of your actions?
- How do you feel if you do that?
- Do you think about the impact of your actions on your relationships, on how you feel, on your life?

5.   Your self.

- Are you hard on yourself?
- Are you always critical of yourself?
- What kinds of things do you say to yourself?
- What tone of voice do you use with yourself?
- Does this tone remind you of anyone?
- Would you speak to someone else like that?
- How does it make you feel when you speak to yourself like that?

"All God's holy people send you their blessings"
...2 Corinthians 13 v 12

Now...Break the chains that bind you...

Your plans, hopes and, dreams can become reality

...but you have to make them happen

God Bless You and give you Peace

References

"Still in Denial" Written by Gerry Rafferty. Published by Metanoia Music ©2021 Produced by Martha Rafferty

[2] 12 Rules for Life. Jordan B Peterson: Allen Lane Publishing: © 2018.

[3] 12 Rules for Life. Jordan B Peterson: Allen Lane Publishing: © 2018.

[4] 12 Rules for Life. Jordan B Peterson: Allen Lane Publishing: © 2018.

[5] 12 Rules for Life. Jordan B Peterson: Allen Lane Publishing: © 2018.

[6] G. Harrison, 'Any Road', from Brainwashed, Dark Horse/ EMI/ Parlophone, © 12th May 2003.

[7] G. Harrison, "Within you, without you". Sgt Pepper's Lonely Hearts Club Band EMI/Parlophone, © 26th May 1967.

[8] 12 Rules for Life. Jordan B Peterson: Allen Lane Publishing: © 2018.

[9] 12 Rules for Life. Jordan B Peterson: Allen Lane Publishing: © 2018.

[10] 12 Rules for Life. Jordan B Peterson: Allen Lane Publishing: © 2018.

[11] 12 Rules for Life. Jordan B Peterson: Allen Lane Publishing: © 2018.

[12] 12 Rules for Life. Jordan B Peterson: Allen Lane Publishing: © 2018.

[13] 12 Rules for Life. Jordan B Peterson: Allen Lane Publishing: © 2018.

[14] 12 Rules for Life. Jordan B Peterson: Allen Lane Publishing: © 2018.

[15] 12 Rules for Life. Jordan B Peterson: Allen Lane Publishing: © 2018.

[16] 12 Rules for Life. Jordan B Peterson: Allen Lane Publishing: © 2018.

[17] 12 Rules for Life. Jordan B Peterson: Allen Lane Publishing: © 2018.

[18] G. Rafferty, "Good Intentions" from the Album Sleepwalking. Published by Liberty/United Records ©

List of UK Organisations offering support (your own country should have similar)

GENERAL

Alcohol Change UK
The national organisation campaigning for effective alcohol policy and improved services for people whose lives are affected by alcohol-related problems.

Beating Addictions
beatingaddictions.co.uk
Information about a range of addictive behaviours and treatments.

Dan 24/7
Free and confidential telephone helpline for anyone in Wales wanting further information or help relating to drugs or alcohol, including families and carers. Phone 0808 808 2234 anytime day or night and they will give you help and advice.

Drink and Drug News (DDN)
Monthly magazine with news, updates and features from across the substance use field. Also produces their rehab guide, a free resource proving information on addiction treatment options.

Drinkline
Advice to those worried about their own, or a loved one's, alcohol use. Contact their free helpline on 0300 123 1110

DrugScience
An independent, science-led drugs charity, bringing together leading drugs experts from a wide range of specialisms to carry out ground-breaking original research into drug harms and effects.

Drugsand.me

Drugsand.me is a social enterprise providing accessible and comprehensive drug education interventions to reduce drug-related harm. Parents' page has a range of advice for parents and carers on how to tackle conversations with kids about drugs, useful links and a downloadable version of their toolkit.

drugwise.org.uk

Formerly DrugScope, DrugWise provides access to evidence-based drug, alcohol and tobacco information and resources, including an international knowledge hub.

FRANK

National drug information service with factfiles and FAQs.

NHS Better Health – Quit smoking

nhs.uk/better-health/quit-smoking

NHS information and advice to help stop smoking.

NHS Choices Alcohol Support

Includes information on alcoholism, binge drinking and caring for someone with an alcohol problem.

NHS Live Well

nhs.uk/livewell

Advice, tips and tools to help with health and wellbeing.

For people experiencing addiction

Sex and Love Addicts Anonymous

07984 977 884 (Infoline)　　slaauk.org

Support groups for people with sex and love addictions.

Stars National Initiative

Support and guidance on parental drug and alcohol misuse

The Samaritans

116 123   24hrs/365days

Turning Point

turning-point.co.uk

Health and social care services in England for people with a learning disability. Also supports people with mental health problems, drug and alcohol abuse or unemployment.

We Are With You

wearewithyou.org.uk

Supports people with drug, alcohol or mental health problems, and their friends and family.

ALCOHOL DEPENDENCY

Alcoholics Anonymous (AA)

0800 9177 650   help@aamail.org (email helpline)

alcoholics-anonymous.org.uk

Help and support for anyone with alcohol problems.

Alcohol Change UK

alcoholchange.org.uk

Information and support options for people worried about how much alcohol they are drinking, in both English and Welsh.

DRUGS DEPENDENCY

Club Drug Clinic

020 3317 3000   clubdrugclinic.cnwl.nhs.uk

Information and support for people worried about their use of recreational drugs.
The clinic offers help in the London boroughs of Kensington & Chelsea,
Hammersmith & Fulham and Westminster.

Cocaine Anonymous UK

0800 612 0225   helpline@cauk.org.uk   cauk.org.uk

Help and support for anyone who wants to stop using cocaine.

DAN 24/7

0808 808 2234   81066 (text DAN)   dan247.org.uk

A bilingual English and Welsh helpline for anyone in Wales in need of further
information or help relating to drugs or alcohol. Also known as the Wales Drug &
Alcohol Helpline.

FRANK

0300 123 6600   talktofrank.com

Confidential advice and information about drugs, their effects and the law.

Marijuana Anonymous

0300 124 0373   helpline@marijuana-anonymous.org.uk
marijuana-anonymous.co.uk

Help for anyone worried about cannabis use.

Narcotics Anonymous

0300 999 1212   ukna.org

Support for anyone who wants to stop using drugs.

GAMING DEPENDENCY

Gamblers Anonymous   gamblersanonymous.org.uk
Support groups for people who want to stop gambling.

Gamcare
0808 8020 133   gamcare.org.uk
Information and support for people who want to stop gambling, including a
helpline and online forum.

National Problem Gambling Clinic
cnwl.nhs.uk/cnwl-national-problem-gambling-clinic
Treats people with gambling problems living in England and Wales aged 16 and
over.

PEOPLE SPECIFIC SUPPORT

PARENTS AND FAMILIES
Adfam   adfam.org.uk
Information and support for friends and family of people with drug or alcohol
problems.

Al-Anon
0800 0086 811   helpline@al-anonuk.org.uk   al-anonuk.org.uk
Offers support meetings across the UK for anyone whose life is affected, or has
been affected, by someone else's drinking. Also provides online support
meetings, and a confidential helpline.

Co-Dependants Anonymous

A set of informal self-help groups made up of people with a common interest in working through the problems that co-dependency has caused in their lives.

Re-Solv

Providing online support and counselling for anyone whose life is affected by volatile substance abuse ('solvent abuse'), including family members and friends.

DrugFAM

Are you affected by someone else's drug or alcohol addiction? Are you bereaved through drug or alcohol use? Contact their free helpline from 9am-9pm, 7 days a week on 0300 888 3853.

Family Lives

Provides help and support for anyone caring for a child.

Families Anonymous

0207 4984 680   famanon.org.uk

Support for friends and family of people with drug problems.

OnlyDads

A national social enterprise that supports parents who are looking to make the best decisions for their family during separation and divorce.

OnlyMums

A national social enterprise that supports parents who are looking to make the best decisions for their family during separation and divorce.

The Icarus Trust

Provide a 'Family & Friends' service. A trained volunteer will provide information and support via email and signpost you to local services.

Relate

Offer advice and relationship counselling for couples, and also provides advice for parents and other family members to help families deal with difficult times.

Scottish Families Affected by Drugs

Work to improve support for families affected by substance use throughout Scotland.

YoungMinds

A children and young people's mental health charity. They have a Parents Helpline Team that offers information, advice and support to any parent/carer who is worried about their child's mental health or emotional wellbeing (up to the age of 25).

Talk About Alcohol

www.talkaboutalcohol.com is written and managed by a charity called The Alcohol Education Trust (AET). The talkaboutalcohol.com site is designed to be used by young people in a classroom setting as part of PSHE lessons on alcohol.

GRANDPARENTS AND KINSHIPS

Grandparents Plus

The national charity which champions the vital role of grandparents, especially when they take on the caring role in difficult family circumstances.

Family Rights Group

Advice for parents and other family members whose children are involved with, or require, social services.

The National Care-line

A voluntary organisation providing information about care and support for older people, their carers and families.

CHILDREN AND YOUNG PEOPLE

Alateen

Run mutual support groups for teenage relatives and friends of alcoholics. Alateen is part of Al-Anon.

NACOA (National Association for the Children of Alcoholics)

Works to address the needs of children growing up in families where one or both parents suffer from alcoholism.

0800 358 3456   helpline@nacoa.org.uk   nacoa.org.uk

Nip in the Bud

Provides films and practical approaches to help parents, teachers, social care staff and others with early recognition of potential mental health conditions in children.

OFFENDERS

Offenders' Families Helpline

The free and confidential national helpline for families of offenders, providing information and advice on all aspects of the criminal justice system.

Release

Release is the national centre of expertise on drugs and drugs law. They provide free, non-judgmental, specialist advice and information to the public and professionals on issues related to drug use and to drug laws.

020 7324 2989 ask@release.org.uk (email helpline)   release.org.uk

DOMESTIC VIOLENCE

Against Violence and Abuse (AVA)

Leading organisation working to end violence against women and girls.

Agenda Alliance

Advocates for change for women and girls at risk.

National Centre for Domestic Violence (NCDV)

Provides a free, fast emergency injunction service to survivors of domestic violence regardless of their financial circumstances, race, gender or sexual orientation.

Refuge

Provide domestic violence advice and helpline for women and children.

Respect

The national organisation for professionals working with people to end their abusive behaviour.

Women's Aid

Women's Aid is the national charity working to end domestic violence against women and children and supports a network of over 500 services across the UK.

BEREAVEMENT

Bereaved through Alcohol and Drugs (BEAD)

Website with information and guidance for anyone that has lost a loved one through drugs or alcohol.   beadproject.org.uk

Child Bereavement UK

Supports families and educates professionals when a baby or child of any age dies or is dying, or when a child is facing bereavement.

Childhood Bereavement Network
The hub for those working with bereaved children, young people and their families across the UK.

Cruse Bereavement Care
Exist to promote the wellbeing of all bereaved people and to enable them to understand their grief and cope with their loss.

Cruse have a section on their website which provides information on drug and alcohol related bereavement.

The Compassionate Friends (TCF)
Provide support to any parent whose child has died. They offer a helpline, an online forum, legal advice and befriending services. They also run a service for bereaved siblings.

The Good Grief Trust
Bereavement support charity with over over 600 local, regional and national bereavement support services listed on their central database of support for those bereaved across the UK.

Widowed and Young (WAY)
Offer support to anyone under 50 who has lost their partner. This may take the form of peer support, practical advice, meet-ups and more.

Winston's Wish
A national charity that supports bereaved children and young people after the death of a significant person. Offer practical bereavement support and guidance to bereaved children and young people up to the age of 25, their families, and the professionals supporting them

About the Author

Paul is a former student of Thornleigh Salesian College Bolton, where he attended as a 6th Former between 1969 and 1972.

He is now a part-time Prison Chaplain at HMP Edinburgh and, was formerly employed by the Ministry of Justice as RC Prison Chaplain at the Category D prison (HMP Thorn Cross) based in Cheshire (UK). The spiritual and pastoral work involves counselling and proactive work to support, care for and, encourage inmates through personal and family crises, which may affect their performance and progress at the prison.

Until its closure, due to Government public sector cuts in 2011, Paul was the last RC Chaplain at HMP Lancaster Castle, a Category C closed conditions prison housed in the Medieval Castle in the centre of Lancaster.

Paul previously worked as News and Programme Producer at Lakeland Radio which was based in Kendal and served the South Lake District area. In 2008 Paul devised, styled and set up a not-for-profit community radio station INDIGO 106.6fm creating its format, branding and delivery from project level to its trusted community status. The small station was based in Kirkby Lonsdale and was twice nominated on a regional basis for its excellence and commitment to serving the welfare of its community. He now produces two online radio stations.

He was previously a Senior Law Lecturer for ten years at Manchester Met University, and later as a Home Office Researcher on the West Yorkshire Burglary Reduction Programme.

He has also published several books on Amazon and Kindle;

the first "St Paul: Life in the Spirit...a yearbook for everyday saints". Also; "St Paul...the Prison Lessons (reflections and insights into Prison Chaplaincy work)" and most recently, "St Paul: The Greatest Songbook..10 songs...10 passages...10 lessons for life"

Paul has a busy personal life which includes an active interest in cycling, swimming, walking and, for his past sins, supporting Bolton Wanderers. He is also actively involved in the local North Berwick community.

◆ ◆ ◆

Also available

By the Author and available from Amazon

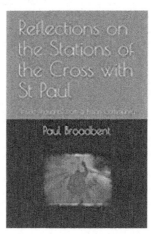

St Paul...a yearbook for everyday saints

Reflections on the Stations of the Cross
Inside thoughts
from a Prison Community

St Paul:The Prison Lessons
Insights into 10 years of Prison Chaplaincy

Rattle that Lock...Break those Chains
...Set yourself free

♦ ♦ ♦

Printed in Great Britain
by Amazon

13147912R00058